THE JOSEPH CALLING

A TWELVE WEEK STUDY

TWELVE WEEK STUDY

THE
JOSEPH
CALLING

6 STAGES TO UNDERSTAND,
NAVIGATE, AND FULFILL YOUR PURPOSE

OS
HILLMAN

ASLAN GROUP
PUBLISHING

INTRODUCTION

God is looking for his sons and daughters to be revealed in the world today. In fact, God has a purpose and destiny for each and every one of us. He has a God-sized assignment for each of us to fulfill on planet earth. But how does one know what that is, and how does God draw us into the larger story of our lives? Perhaps you've even wondered, "Can I know these things?" The answer to this question is a resounding yes!

Most of us know God calls individuals into a specific assignment, but few of us know the processes by which he does it. The Joseph calling is a unique process that not all people will experience, but it is a verifiable process God takes people through to achieve a higher purpose for their lives. This process of discovery led me to discover six unique stages that Josephs must pass through in order to understand, navigate, and fulfill their destinies.

I have found that few people know their purpose and why God has put them on the earth in the first place. These are the issues I will address in this book—I want to help readers reconcile adversity and crisis with destiny and purpose. This book will reveal the six critical stages God's modern-day Josephs, almost without exception, experience in their destination toward the larger story of their lives. I've been able to document these stages in the lives of almost every major character in the Bible and in those whom God has used greatly in his kingdom in modern society.

When we understand God's processes, we're more likely to embrace his truths, and subsequently desire a deeper relationship with him. Welcome to the journey. I am confident you won't be the same person after you learn these six critical stages to fulfill your calling.

Ultimately, God is looking to make known his intention to use leaders to accomplish his plan on the earth today. Whether you're young or old, there's a plan of God for you at every stage of life. You will learn the signposts of calling and how to respond to them. You will learn from the biblical stories and the modern-day case studies of those who have gone before us. You will learn the 6 stages to discover, navigate and fulfill your purpose. God wants to reveal to you your purpose, why he made you, and why he sent you into this world. He wants you to know his unique assignment for you—and only you—to fulfill on planet earth.

This 12-week study will allow you to study, reflect and share the key truths from *The Joseph Calling* book. I encourage you to form a small group of four to eight participants to gain the most from this 12-week study. May God use this time to help you understand, navigate and fulfill your purpose.

HOW TO HAVE AN EFFECTIVE SMALL GROUP STUDY

A friend of mine who is an orthodontist told me of a time when God led him to begin a Bible study on Monday mornings. He and his friend, another dentist, were to partner on the Bible study. Monday morning arrived and the two men were prepared to greet all those who had been invited to come. Ten minutes had gone by and no one had showed up. The dentist friend said, "Well, I guess we should just postpone until next week." My orthodontist friend replied, "Oh, no. It is time to begin. God told us to have this study. So, we must be good stewards and begin our study right now. My friend began to teach the Bible study to an empty room. Within the hour, men and women began to file into the room for the Monday morning gathering. By the end of the hour, several were in the room. Now, if my friends had decided to leave at that moment of doubt, they would have missed God for that day.

Many years later Oswald Chambers found himself in the same position when launching a Bible school. God told him to begin the school. The first day he had one student. But by the end of the first month, he was almost full.

PRAYER: THE FIRST STEP

Friend, the first thing you need to determine is whether God is leading you to begin a small group. Spend time seeking God's direction for such a gathering. Oswald Chambers said, "Much of Christian enterprise is Ishmael, seeking to do God's will in our own way—the one thing Jesus Christ never did." It is important to follow the guidance of the Holy Spirit in all we do. If we will do this, then we will birth something from the Spirit of God, not from our own effort. Once you have confirmation of direction, take the next step as He shows you.

FACILITATOR VERSUS TEACHER

Once you have a place and time selected, it is important follow some basic principles in leading a small group.

Consider yourself a facilitator more than a teacher. This study guide is designed to provide the teaching necessary for the lesson. Your role is to create an atmosphere for learning and applying what is in the lesson. The lesson is designed to take up thirty to forty-five minutes of time. You can always expand with additional scriptures, questions, or comments from group members. You can also expand by having more time for prayer needs. Group participation is the key to having a successful group.

Open your time with prayer and ask God to lead your study. The Holy Spirit wants to lead your time. Let Him work. You will be amazed what God will do if you set the table for others to eat from.

After your time of study, have a few minutes for specific prayer for the members. This environment should be a safe place to share needs and get involved in the lives of the members of the group. The only reason you may not want to do this is if your group gets too large. However, if your group is less than ten or even fifteen, you should allow for this.

There are a few things you will want to stay away from when conducting a small group. If you are hosting a group with many different denominations represented, avoid negative comments about a particular denomination. Also, stay away from divisive topics that cannot be adequately addressed in a small group. There will be times when some questions arise that cannot be adequately addressed in the time you have together. Tell that person you will address their issue after your study time. Finally, you may have seekers join your group. We are all at different stages of our spiritual journeys. If you know you have unbelievers or new Christians in your group, stay away from religious language that these people may not be familiar with. Be sensitive to where people are.

We pray this study and future studies will be a blessing to you and those you serve. Let us know how we can improve these studies. Feel free to send us suggestions and comments.

CAN I KNOW MY PURPOSE?

"May He grant you according to your heart's desire, and fulfill all your purpose." —Psalm 20:4 NKJV

"... everything got started in him and finds its purpose in him." —Colossians 1:16 MSG

READ CHAPTER 1, 2, AND 3

Summary: In this chapter Os Hillman tells about his journey and how he discovered his purpose. He cites that most people do not understand their purpose. He believes that everyone can know their purpose. He also says purpose and vocation are not necessarily the same. Your purpose can be lived out in many different ways.

QUESTIONS

1. How would you define purpose? Consider the verses below.
Read the following verses before answering: Jeremiah 1:5, Matthew 6:33, John 15:16, Jeremiah 9:23, Psalm 138:8, Psalm 16:5,6, Acts 17:26

2. Is purpose and knowing why God made you the same? How does vocation relate to one's purpose? Explain the difference and the implications.

Read Ephesians 2:10, Revelation 2:17, Romans 11:29

3. What was Jesus' purpose?

Read John 3:16, 1 John 3:8, John 5:30, John 18:37

Hint: Each of these verses reveals a specific purpose he fulfilled.

4. What are the steps recommended in chapter 2 to discover your purpose and why God made you? List your 10 most unique attributes below.

1. _____

2. _____

3. _____

4. _____

5. _____

6. _____

7. _____

8. _____

9. _____

10. _____

5. Complete the exercise recommended by the author in chapter 2. After completing the exercise write the statement below you came up with based on your top 4 attributes.

What is one thing you will do because of what you learned in this chapter?

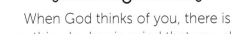

When God thinks of you, there is
something he has in mind that you alone
are uniquely qualified to do for God.

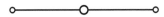

UNDERSTANDING THE JOSEPH CALLING

"As they pass through the Valley of Baka (trouble), they make it a spring; the rain also covers it with pools." —Psalm 84:6

READ CHAPTER 4 AND 5

Summary: In these two chapters Os explains what a Joseph Calling is and why it is important to understand this unique calling from God. You will gain a better understanding of why and how God uses adversity in the lives of his leaders. You will learn why a crisis is often the entry door to the larger story of your life. In this process of discovering, navigating, and fulfilling our purpose in life, we may find ourselves in situations or required to do work we never wanted to do, yet God gives us favor even in that place. This is true for many modern-day Josephs who are displaced from their past careers due to the economic climate in which we live, but they realize God's favor is with them in the "prison" in which they find themselves. There may be destruction all around us, but God will preserve our lives.

QUESTIONS

1. Joseph's story has several components that are key to his training ground to become a the second most powerful man in Egypt to be a spiritual and spiritual provider for others. These key stages are 1) dream/crisis, 2) character development, 3) isolation, 4) betrayal, 5) problem solving, 6) network. Describe each of these stages and the character God was trying to develop in Joseph through each stage.

1. _____

_____

2. _____

_____

3. _____

_____

4. _____

_____

5. _____

_____

6. _____

_____

2. God releases his blessing in proportion to the character you allow him to develop within you. Explain what you think this means.

3. In the valley, it is more difficult to see ahead; the clouds often cover the valley and limit our sight. Joseph was thrust into a deep valley that left him wondering if the God of his fathers had forsaken him. Jesus hoped that he might be able to avoid the valley that caused him to sweat drops of blood, hoping there would be another way besides going to the cross. There is a valley that each of us must enter, usually unwillingly, in order to experience the God of the valley—and to experience his faithfulness in the valleys. What are some temptations often encountered when walking through a valley experience? What do you think Joseph thought about God during his valley experience?

4. The apostle Paul understood this process when he wrote: "We are troubled on every side, yet not distressed; we are perplexed, but not in despair; persecuted, but not forsaken; cast down, but not destroyed; always bearing about in the body the dying of the Lord Jesus, that the life also of Jesus might be made manifest in our body. For we which live are always delivered unto death for Jesus' sake, that the life also of Jesus might be made manifest in our mortal flesh. So then death worketh in us, but life in you." (2 Corinthians 4:8–12 KJV). What are some observations you can make about the way the apostle Paul views adversity that others find difficult to do?

5. Swiss businessman Juerg Opprecht is a modern-day Joseph. Describe some of the events of his life that contributed to him becoming a Joseph.

What is one thing you will do because of what you learned in this chapter?

God releases his blessing in proportion
to the character we allow him to develop
in us. God will totally ruin us and remake
us at the same time.

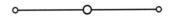

ADVERSITY IS A KEY COMPONENT OF A JOSEPH CALLING

"But as for you, you meant evil against me; but God meant it for good, in order to bring it about as it is this day, to save many people alive." —Genesis 50:20

READ CHAPTER 5 AND 6

Summary: Like the twelve men who had to go across the Jordan before Joshua, who got wet and muddy, so everyone to whom is given the Joseph calling must endure hardship so that many others who will come behind may enter their spiritual Promised Land. This is the special calling for God's Josephs. It may involve betrayal just as Joseph and Jesus experienced; it may require losing all your earthly possessions; it may even require losing relationships dear to you. But you must be able to say as Joseph said, "You meant it for evil, but God meant it for good." Why? "So that I would be sent ahead for your benefit and others coming behind me." God tells us that all things will work together for good in the end (Romans 8:28).

QUESTIONS

1. Jesus is the only person who made plan A; but for the rest of us, God turns our plan B and C into his plan A. How do we see this being played out in the life of Joseph?

2. The Joseph process is a circumcision and baptism process that is personal, painful, and bloody. It is messy, but it is also necessary. God is picky with his leaders. He almost killed Moses because he refused to circumcise his child after eighty years of preparation. Moses prepared for forty years in Egypt, being educated and trained, learning the ways of the nation he would have to relate to forty years later; then he spent another forty years tending sheep and being alone in the fields (isolation). All of this was preparing Moses for his assignment. What can we learn from these isolation and waiting times when it comes to being significantly used by God?

3. It is not enough to teach people or be taught; they must also be engaged in the battle. When the disciples went out the first time, they were amazed that even the demons responded to them. There is always a trumpet call that requires a leader to step into the larger story where he or she can experience the power of God. Knowledge without experience is fruitless. David said in Psalm 144:1 "He trains my hands for war." Explain what this means in the context of David's and Joseph's life and perhaps your own life.

4. Every leader God used discovered there was a time and moment that was a turning point in his or her life:
- Moses at the burning bush.
- Noah's instructions to build the ark.
- Gideon called to destroy the idols.
- Esther called to save the nation.
- Paul called to the Gentiles.
- Peter called to lead the church.

Can you cite a time in your life that became the trumpet call or beginnings of the larger story of your life? If so, how has that event impacted your life.

5. Often our initial vision must go through a death process before it can become God's vision. God's vision begins its first stage through a crisis. For Joseph, it was being thrown into a pit to be sold as a slave.

This would lead him into his character-building season, which is the second stage, that would last for thirteen long years. His original vision had to die in order for God's vision to be fulfilled. Why do you think the original vision had to die first? Have you ever had a death of a vision in your life? Has it been resurrected in a different way? Explain.

What is one thing you will do because of what you learned in this chapter?

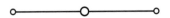

God often puts us through the experience and discipline of darkness to teach us to hear and obey him. We can then become his messengers as he births a message through our life experiences.

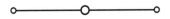

CRISIS IS OFTEN THE FRONT DOOR OF YOUR LARGER STORY

"For He Himself has said, 'I will never leave you nor forsake you.'" —Hebrews 13:5

READ CHAPTER 6

Summary: Before we enter the first stage of the Joseph calling, the crisis stage, there is often a dream or vision of what we believe God may be calling us to do. Joseph had a dream that indicated something was going to happen in his future. He did not totally understand his dream, but that dream had a devastating impact on his life when he publicly shared it with his brothers, who demonstrated that they could not handle it.

Joseph was immature and lacked wisdom at this stage of his life. His brothers perceived him as the favored son at their expense—he got a beautiful coat the others did not get, and so his brothers became jealous of Joseph's favoritism. His dream was from God, but his handling of it showed an immaturity that God was going to use to create a new Joseph and save a nation through him. God used this dream to usher him into the crisis stage.

QUESTIONS

1. When Joseph was thrown into the pit, it ushered in a crisis that must have created a level of fear Joseph had never known before. He was thrust from one place in life to a whole new place, with no rights or choices, and, no doubt, with a questioning of God's love. "Where is my God? How could he let this happen to me? What happened to the dream I received from God?" What are some common responses we often have when a crisis takes place in our lives? What should we do when faced with a crisis?

2. There is a time within the crisis stage that all Josephs experience, which I call the black hole. It usually comes in the first phase of your crisis. The black hole is a time when all of life is disrupted and you have no ability to do anything about it. You may lose your finances or your health or even your job. Life is kicked out from under you. It is like being thrown into a rowboat with no oars and the boat has small holes in it. You are simply waiting for the boat to fill up with water and you fear you will go down with it. Sometimes what you fear comes to pass, but other times God takes you through a process that reveals his activity in your circumstances and provides for you in a supernatural way. Have you ever been in a "black hole" period in your life? Explain. What does Os say one should do if they enter the black hole?

3. Another aspect of the black hole is God's seeming sabotage of your ability to complete the task during this season. Nothing is more frustrating than carrying out a task and having your superior thwart your efforts to do what he or she asked you to do. Moses must have felt this way after God told him to go to Pharaoh and tell him to release the people of Israel. He said, "I am going to give you the power to release the children of Israel by the miracles I will do through you." Yet at the same time, he told Moses they would not be released because he was going to put a hard heart in Pharaoh: "The LORD said to Moses, 'When you return to Egypt, see that you perform before Pharaoh all the wonders I have given you the power to do. But I will harden his heart so that he will not let the people go'" (Exodus 4:21). How do we reconcile this? Why does God sometimes delay answering our prayers?

4. Oswald Chambers said, "Whenever God gives a vision to a Christian, it is as if He puts him in 'the shadow of His hand'" (Isaiah 49:2). The saint's duty is to be still and listen. There is a "darkness" that comes from too much light—that is the time to listen. The story of Abram and Hagar in Genesis 16 is an excellent example of listening to so-called good advice during a time of darkness, rather than waiting for God to send the light.

What should you do when God seems far away? What has God promised regarding never leaving us or forsaking us?
Read Hebrews 13:5.

5. Friend, you may feel like you are in prison; you may feel stuck in your circumstances. Let God meet you in this place. Let this be a time of discovering the power and presence of God during adverse circumstances. Sometimes the winds of adversity force us to adjust our sails to capture a different kind of wind. What should be our response when we are faced with a crisis? How does Satan tempt us during times of crisis?
Read Romans 8:28, 1 Peter 1:6–9, 1 Corinthians 13:12.

What is one thing you will do because of what you learned in this chapter?

Those who fulfill the larger story of their lives are rarely looking to do just that; it happens when a crisis takes place. The crisis becomes the front door to the larger story of his or her life.

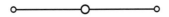

6 STAGES TO UNDERSTAND, NAVIGATE AND FULFILL YOUR PURPOSE

"But as for you, you meant evil against me; but God meant it for good, in order to bring it about as it is this day, to save many people alive." —Genesis 50:20

READ CHAPTER 7

Summary: There are six stages God uses in the life of all Josephs that include 1) Recruitment/Crisis, 2) Character Development, 3) Isolation, 4) Cross/Betrayal, 5) Problem Solving and 6) Networks. In today's lesson we will look at Joseph's 6 unique stages.

QUESTIONS

1. Joseph's 6 stages can be seen in the following events.

1. *Crisis* – His brothers sell him into slavery
2. *Isolation* – He is sent away from his family and is alone. He is later imprisoned.
3. *Character development* – He went through 13 years of trial that removed all pride from his life.

4. *Cross* – He is betrayed by his brothers.

5. *Problem Solving* – He solves a famine problem for Pharaoh and the nation of Israel and he saves an entire nation from starvation.

6. *Network* – The 12 tribes of Israel are saved from death and become a nation.

What observations can you make about how God used these 6 stages in the life of Joseph?

2. When Joseph was thrown into the pit, it ushered in a crisis that must have created a level of fear Joseph had never known before. He was thrust from one place in life to a whole new place, with no rights or choices, and, no doubt, with a questioning of God's love. "Where is my God? How could he let this happen to me? What happened to the dream I received from God?" What response should we have when we are faced with a crisis?

3. The Black Hole is the best and worst of times. It is the worst for obvious reasons, but it can be the best because you begin to see the activity of God show up in the most unusual ways. You have a heightened sense of his activity in your life after the initial black hole stage. Oswald Chambers said, "Whenever God gives a vision to a Christian, it is as if He puts him in "the shadow of His hand" (Isaiah 49:2). The saint's duty is to be still and listen." What are some ways we can better listen to God's voice in our lives?

4. There is a time for everything. If God has called you to some endeavor and you are   frustrated that it has not manifested yet, know that times of preparation and simmering are required before the vision can be achieved. Seldom does God call and manifest the vision at the same time. There is preparation. There is testing. There is relationship building that must take place between you and God. Only once this is complete will you see the vision materialize. Have you ever gone through such a time? If so, describe what God did in your life through that experience. If you are in such a time now, what do you see God doing in your life? What have you learned about yourself?

5. Stage three often leads us into isolation. Joseph was isolated from his family and all that he knew. This stage can also be described as the desert stage. When the Israelites were freed from slavery, they had to pass through the desert. The word desert comes from a Hebrew word *midbaar*, which means "to speak." Hosea 2:14 tell us, "Therefore I am now going to allure her; I will lead her into the wilderness and speak tenderly to her."

What are some characteristics of the desert?

What is one thing you will do because of what you learned in this chapter?

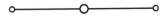

I have concluded that most of us couldn't enter the larger story of our lives without the help of a significant disruption.

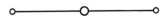

STAGE 1: GOD OFTEN RECRUITS HIS SERVANTS THROUGH A CRISIS

"Jesus learned obedience through the things he suffered."
—Hebrew 5:11

READ CHAPTER 7 AND 8

Summary: Whenever God takes us through the land of affliction, he will do two things through that affliction: First, he will bring such healing that we will be able to forget the pain, and second, he will make us fruitful from the painful experiences. God does not waste our afflictions if we allow him the freedom to complete the work within us. His desire is to create virtue that remains during the times of testing so that he can bring us into the place of fruitfulness. He has never promised to keep us from entering the valleys of testing, but he promised to make us fruitful in them.

QUESTIONS

1. In chapter 7 Os describes three reasons a person might go through adversity. Cite those reasons. Which ones can you relate to personally?

2. Many leaders in whom God used significantly were ushered into their larger story through a crisis. What was the crisis that began the journey to their larger story for each of these leaders.

a. Abraham

b. Joseph

c. David

d. Martin Luther

e. Martin Luther King, Jr.

f. Esther.

3. Every call from God is extraordinary; however, not every call is high profile. We may not affect the masses, but we are all called to a unique assignment from God. The depth and width of our adversity often determines the level of influence we will have. How do we see this in the life of Paul played out? What can we learn from this we can apply to our lives?

4. God turned Os Hillman's valley of trouble into a door of hope for hundreds of thousands of people around the world by leading him to begin writing about his experiences. This led to writing *TGIF: Today God Is First*, a daily devotional that is read by hundreds of thousands of people each day in over a hundred nations. It has also taken him to twenty-six nations to teach and equip men and women in the body of Christ. God turned his mess into messages and made him a messenger. God ushered him into his larger story through a personal and business crisis. What can we learn from this and other examples in this chapter about the way God works in the lives of his people?

5. There is a time in the life of every leader when the trumpet sounds. It is up to us to step into the larger story by sensing the moment and allowing God to move us into that story. It will never be comfortable or convenient at the time. Let me encourage you to consider your life circumstance as a possible trumpet blast that might bring you into the larger story of your life. Friend, God may take you through times when you will question his love. In such times, you must cling to his coattails so that you see his purposes in it. Do not throw away your confidence; it will be richly rewarded.

> "You need to persevere so that when you have done the will of God, you will receive what he has promised. For, "In just a very little while, he who is coming will come and will not delay. But My righteous one will live by faith. And I take no pleasure in the one who shrinks back" (Hebrews 10:36–38).

Are you going through a crisis? It may be that God has just begun the process of the Joseph calling in your life. What is the writer of Hebrews exhorting us to do in Hebrews 10:36-38?

What is one thing you will do because of what you learned in this chapter?

Sometimes we must get to a deep
level of pain and disappointment in order
to motivate us toward real change.
The pain to remain the same must
exceed the pain to change. We don't
want just a habit change; we want a real
transformational nature change.

STAGE 2: CHARACTER DEVELOPMENT—GOD DEVELOPS HIS SERVANTS THROUGH A SERIES OF CHARACTER TESTS

"As far as the east is from the west, so far has he removed our transgressions from us." —Psalm 103:12

READ CHAPTER 9

Summary: Joseph went through a thirteen-year season of character building and preparation. It was hardly an "assignment" that matched his purpose. His primary assignment to fulfill God's call included this painful process. God takes many leaders through a season of character building that often has little to do with their natural gifts, but it is a vital step toward developing the character that God requires for the assignment he has for that person.

QUESTIONS

1. Name a time in your life when God was working on your character. What was the situation before and what was the result later?

2. Peter was an impulsive man. He responded quickly to situations without thinking of the consequences. He often responded to Jesus only to have to repent for not following through on his commitments. Jesus even rebuked satan in Peter when Peter argued with the Lord about Jesus' future death. He told Jesus he would never betray him, but then went on to betray him three times in the twenty-four-hour period just before Jesus' crucifixion. What allowed Peter to mature in character? How is he different later in his life?

3. A test always follows a victory. Such was the case for Jesus. The Bible says that the Spirit of God drove Jesus into the wilderness right after his baptism and the Father's audible proclamation of Jesus as the Son of God (Mark 1:11). Jesus was led to the desert by the Spirit to be tempted by satan during his forty days of fasting in the wilderness. He was tempted in three core areas. Name these three areas. How are we tested in similar ways?

4. Sometimes God frustrates our desire to experience him to deepen our experience in him. God's process often involves failing miserably at something, learning the lesson or lessons of the failure, walking in the new truth successfully, and then teaching it to others. It becomes our authority from which we minister to others. Failure is often God's greatest tool for success in the kingdom. Name a time in your life where you learned a significant lesson through a failure.

5. Observe how Jesus dealt with failure in his disciples. When he revealed himself to them after the resurrection, he did not shame them or communicate his disappointment with them. When he saw them for the first time, he said to them, "Peace be with you." He did not say, "Hey, you guys all betrayed me. What's up with that?"

When the angel of the Lord came to Gideon in the wheat press, he said, "Oh, mighty warrior!" Gideon at that time was a fearful, angry-at-God farmer simply trying to avoid being killed by his enemies. God always looks at what we are becoming, not at what we are. He does not look at our past or our current condition, but he sees his plans for us. How comforting this is to know about the nature of God. Satan always defines our lives based on our past; God defines us by our future. In what ways have we had a flawed perception of God's view towards us, especially in regard to our failures?

What is one thing you will do because of what you learned in this chapter?

God often allows us to go low
in order to go high with God.

STAGE 3: ISOLATION— GOD ISOLATES HIS LEADERS TO TURN MESSES INTO MESSAGES AND MESSENGERS

"I will give you hidden treasure, riches stored in secret places, so that you may know that I am the LORD, the God of Israel, who summons you by name." —Isaiah 45:3

READ: CHAPTER 10

Summary: Stage three of our six stages to understand, navigate, and fulfill your destiny is the isolation stage. It is a time when we become isolated and often experience deep feelings of loneliness and abandonment. If we are not careful at this stage, this time can be dangerous to our psyche, and we can fall prey to many kinds of sin in an effort to cope. However, it can be a fruitful season if we allow God to enter that time with us.

The apostle Paul tells us in Galatians of some of the facts surrounding his own conversion. He clearly understood the call Jesus placed on his life—he did not have to consult with others about this calling. But before he was released to begin his own mission, he went to Arabia for three years and stayed in the desert. Why did Paul have to go to Arabia for three years before he ever met another disciple of Jesus Christ? The Bible does not tell us plainly why Paul spent three years in Arabia. However, based upon many examples of God placing special calls on individuals' lives, we know it often requires a time of separation between the old life and the new one. No doubt, Paul had plenty of time to consider what had taken place in his heart, and so he had time to develop an intimate knowledge and relationship with his newfound Savior. His life was about to change dramatically. Isolation is a stage for many of God's leaders to turn messes into messages and messengers.

QUESTIONS

1. David was forced to hide in the Cave of Adullam. He wrote Psalm 34, 57 and 142 during his time in the cave. What do we learn about David's state of mind while he was in the cave?

2. David was a man looking for purpose in all of his struggles. He probably wondered how he got from being a king's favored son to being an outlaw and having to fake madness just to stay alive. He probably thought often of the day when Samuel anointed him as the next king of Israel as a teen. How do we reconcile the God we want with the God who IS that seems to contradict what we thought about God's ways? How have your views of God changed by understanding the 6 stages of a call from God?

3. God doesn't allow us to remain in our cave of isolation for too long. If we remain there too long, we become defeated by our circumstances. It is interesting what the prophet told David to do: "But the prophet Gad said to David, 'Do not stay in the stronghold. Go into the land of Judah'" (1 Samuel 22:5). What does the land of Judah mean? What are we to conclude about this instruction?

4. God used the mess of the cave to turn David into one of our greatest messengers, who wrote much of the Psalms, which have comforted millions of people over the centuries. We learn the lessons from tears he shed in these times, and they are a spring from which we deeply drink: "As they pass through the Valley of Baka (weeping), they make it a place of springs; the autumn rains also cover it with pools. They go from strength to strength, till each appears before God in Zion" (Psalm 84:6–7). We realize that it is only the Lord who can illumine our path during these dark times: "You, LORD, are my lamp; the LORD turns my darkness into light" (2 Samuel 22:29). What do these verses and the example of David tell us about the process God's uses to raise up His best leaders?

5. If God calls us into darkness in order to enter his presence, then that darkness will become an entry to new levels of relationship with a God who longs for fellowship with us. God was testing David's mettle and preparing him for a new chapter in his life. Charles Swindoll describes the role that isolation and the cave may play in a believer's journey:

David has been brought to the place where God can truly begin to shape him and use him. When the sovereign God brings us to nothing, it is to reroute our life, not to end it. Human perspective says, "Aha, you've lost this, you've lost that. You've caused this, you've caused that. You've ruined this, you've ruined that. End your life!" But God says, "No. No. You're in the cave. But that doesn't mean it's curtains. That means it's time to reroute your life. Now's the time to start anew!" That's exactly what He does with David.

Who did God bring into David's life while he was still in the cave? What was the result?

What is one thing you will do because of what you learned in this chapter?

God turns our messes into
messages and messengers.

THE CROSS—EVERY LEADER MUST EXPERIENCE THE CROSS THROUGH BETRAYAL

"Blessed are you when people insult you, persecute you and falsely say all kinds of evil against you because of me." —Matthew 5:11

"But if you do not forgive others their sins, your Father will not forgive your sins." —Matthew 6:15

READ CHAPTER 11

Summary: The fourth stage of the Joseph calling, for helping to understand, navigate, and fulfill your purpose, is the cross. There appears to be an unwritten spiritual law that God requires of leaders in whom he uses significantly in his kingdom. I call it the graduate level test. This test contributes more to a leader coming to his or her own personal cross than any other activity.

Many who have matured in their faith journey needed help to get to that maturity. There are certain experiences God allows that are designed to bring us to the absolute end of our carnal lives. This is so that Christ fully lives through us. Even the best of saints are unable to crucify the flesh by themselves. We might be able to put two nails into our own cross, but it always takes someone else to drive in the third one. And that usually involves some type of betrayal in the life of the leader.

Most of the great leaders in the Bible experienced some form of betrayal:

- For Moses, it was Korah.
- For Job, it was his three friends.
- For Jesus, it was Judas.
- For David, it was Absalom.
- For Joseph, it was his brothers and Potiphar's wife.

QUESTIONS

1. Betrayals seem to be evident in almost every leader's life at some point along their journey. What is the test of a betrayal? What does God require us to do?
Read 2 Corinthians 4:11–12

2. What does Jesus say He will do if we do not forgive others?
See Matthew 5:11; Matthew 6:15; Matthew 5:43–48

3. What would be an example of applying the principle of "washing the feet of our Judas?" What practical action steps might this involve?

4. "If your enemy is hungry, feed him; if he is thirsty, give him something to drink. In doing this, you will heap burning coals on his head" (Romans 12:20). What affect does Jesus say following this instruction will have on our betrayer? What will be the benefit to you?

5. You should know that forgiveness is as much for you as it is for your offender. Until you forgive, you will remain in a prison cell. True forgiveness of those who wrong us demonstrates more than anything else whether or not you are serious about walking with God at a deeper level. Ask God if there is anyone in your life you need to forgive. Write their name down here:

Are you willing to forgive them? If so, tell God you forgive them.

What is one thing you will do because of what you learned in this chapter?

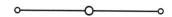

We might be able to put two nails
into our own cross, but it always takes
someone else to drive in the third one.

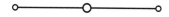

PROBLEM SOLVING: YOU ARE CALLED TO SOLVE A PROBLEM

"Dear friends, do you think you'll get anywhere in this if you learn all the right words but never do anything? Does merely talking about faith indicate that a person really has it?... Isn't it obvious that God-talk without God-acts is outrageous nonsense?" —James 2:14, 17 MSG

"For we are His workmanship, created in Christ Jesus for good works, which God prepared beforehand that we should walk in them." —Ephesians 2:10

READ CHAPTER 12

Summary: The fifth stage, the problem-solving stage, is a key component of the six stages of the Joseph calling. Once God has taken you through a process of maturity, then the fruit of that process often results in you solving some type of problem that ultimately gives you the authority in which God wants you to operate.

For example, God raised up Pharaoh in order to demonstrate

his power to him, his nation, and the people of Israel (Romans 9:17). Through Moses, God solved the problem of freeing the people of Israel from slavery, using as the catalyst a series of miraculous plagues. This is how God works through us to bring solutions that can solve problems in our world. We gain influence by being better and by providing solutions to culture's leaders and their problems. And when there are injustices, we tap into the power of God for the solution to the injustice, just as Martin Luther King Jr. did. It may cost you your life when you stand up for righteousness and a cause that is bigger than yourself.

QUESTIONS

1. Johannes Gutenberg was a German goldsmith and inventor best known for inventing the Gutenberg press in 1455. What problem did he solve and what was its impact on society?

2. People can't hear when our negative actions speak louder than our actual words. Instead of being critics of culture we need to be solving problems in culture. Are there any actions that are hindering your words? Someone once said, "People don't care what you know; they just want to know that you care." What impact does problem solving have in the context of these two statements?

3. Culture does not care who solves their problem. They just want their problem solved. If you solve a problem in a person's life you gain influence. How did Jesus model this? Give some examples.

4. When satan throws bricks at you, let God use them to build his kingdom by tapping into heaven and letting God solve the problem. Jesus never fretted over a problem; He already has a solution. So too do you, because Jesus lives inside of you. Solving problems will give you greater authority and influence. When Jesus told the disciples to feed the five thousand, he enabled them to fulfill the assignment. God enables what he instructs us to do! What should be our attitude toward our next problem?

5. George Washington Carver is one of the greatest inspirational stories of all time. Here was a man who should have been a victim to his circumstances. He lived during the worst time of slavery in America. He lost his mother to the slave trade; he was discriminated against continually. He could have become a victim to his circumstances. Yet he was a follower of Jesus who was gifted with an inventive mind. He discovered more than three hundred uses for the peanut and one hundred uses for the sweet potato that transformed the Southern economy. How did God use Carver to solve a problem? What was the result?

What is one thing you will do because of what you learned in this chapter?

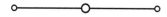

During your desert time, God gives
you a message or a solution to a problem
that he will use to serve others.
It becomes your authority from which
you minister to others.

NETWORKS—GOD WORKS THROUGH UNIFIED NETWORKS TO BUILD HIS KINGDOM

"The LORD said, 'If as one people speaking the same language they have begun to do this, then nothing they plan to do will be impossible for them.'" —Genesis 11:6

"Five will chase a hundred, but a hundred will chase ten thousand." —Leviticus 26:8

"Though one may be overpowered, two can defend themselves. A cord of three strands is not quickly broken." —Ecclesiastes 4:12

"How could one man chase a thousand, or two put ten thousand to flight ...?" —Deuteronomy 32:30

READ CHAPTER 13

Summary: The sixth stage of the call of God in the life of a leader involves networks. One of the great values of God we see in the Scriptures is the need for groups of people to come together in unity for a cause greater than any single person could accomplish by him- or herself.

God reveals this value for unity in diversity in the Trinity—Father, Son, and Holy Spirit. Each member of the Trinity has a particular role to play. And when Jesus decided to start his worldwide mission, he recruited twelve disciples to accomplish this task. Interestingly enough, these were recruited from average men from the marketplace, not from the clergy of the day. Jesus spent three years pouring into these men and building unity among them for a common mission.

Not only that, but Daniel had a small group of men he relied on to share the burdens they had as people living in Babylon serving an ungodly king. When Nebuchadnezzar told Daniel that he had to tell him his dream and interpret it or else he would die, Daniel immediately went to his core circle of friends—Shadrach, Meshach, and Abednego—to pray together. God answered their prayer, and Daniel's life, and the lives of the men in his administration, were spared. God's name was uplifted in the whole kingdom as a result of this miracle. In this lesson we will discuss the value of networks and how God uses them to accomplish His purposes.

QUESTIONS

1. What was Daniel's network? Why was it important for Daniel to have his network?

2. William Wilberforce was credited for abolishing slavery in England after 30 years of work. However, it was his network of leaders called The Clapham Group who collaborated to impact social injustices in England. What were some characteristics of their network?

3. Early in Os Hillman's marketplace call, God placed John 17:21-23 deeply into his spirit. Let's look at it for a moment. Jesus prayed:

> "My prayer is not for them alone. I pray also for those who will believe in me through their message, that all of them may be one, Father, just as you are in me and I am in you. May they also be in us so that the world may believe that you have sent me. I have given them the glory that you gave me, that they may be one as we are one—I in them and you in me—so that they may be brought to complete unity. Then the world will know that you sent me and have loved them even as you have loved me." —John 17:20-23

How might we apply this verse today in the context of our work and among Christian activity today?

4.   God is waiting for his sons and daughters to step into their true destinies. Read Romans 8:19. What do you think Paul is exhorting us to do in this verse?

5. God has been preparing his marketplace followers to be a part of an end-time harvest of souls. There is a church that has been sleeping, but they are getting aroused as we see more and more of our spiritual foundations eroding. For the first time in many years, we are beginning to see the remnant have righteous anger to be part of the solution to bring God back into our nation.

> "Proclaim this among the nations:
> Prepare for war!
> Rouse the warriors!
> Let all the fighting men draw near and attack.
> Beat your plowshares into swords
> and your pruning hooks into spears.
> Let the weakling say,
> "I am strong!"
> Come quickly, all you nations from every side,
> And assemble there.
> Bring down your warriors, LORD!" —Joel 3:9–11

What is Joel saying when he says, "Beat your plowshares into swords and your pruning hooks into spears"? What is the application to us today? What does this verse seem to indicate about the last days?

What is one thing you will do because of what you learned in this chapter?

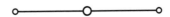

Networks are always necessary to
create change in culture.

THERE IS A TRUMPET CALL FOR EVERY BELIEVER TO ENTER THEIR LARGER STORY

"For the earnest expectation of the creation eagerly waits for the revealing of the sons of God." —Romans 8:19

READ CHAPTERS 14, 15, 16, 17 AND 18

Summary: Most of us couldn't enter the larger story of our lives without the help of a significant disruption.

QUESTIONS

1. Cite the events of the 6 stages of Moses' life:

1. Recruitment: _____

_____

2. Character Development: _____

_____

3. Isolation: _____

_____

4. Betrayal: _____

_____

5. Problem Solving: _____

_____

6. Networks: _____

_____

2. Name the 6 stages of Jacob's life:

1. Recruitment: _____

_____

2. Character Development: _____

_____

3. Isolation: _____

_____

4. Betrayal: _____

_____

5. Problem Solving: _____

_____

6. Networks: _____

_____

3. Name the 6 stages of Paul's life:

1. Recruitment:

2. Character Development:

3. Isolation:

4. Betrayal:

5. Problem Solving:

6. Networks:

4. The purpose of the six stages of the Joseph calling is designed to usher you into the larger story of your life. That larger story should be a life that is filled with the activity of God and the manifest presence of his life being lived through you. Henry Blackaby developed a popular Bible study series in 1990. The premise of the study was based on seven core principles about how God relates to his people. The very first principle was that God is always at work around us; our responsibility is to join in what he is already doing. We are not to think up things to do for God; rather, we are to join him in what he wants to do and what he is already doing in the earth today. Where do you see God working in your life right now? Is there a larger story He may be wanting to create in your life? What might that look like?

5. What were some examples God showing up in the life of Os Hillman? What do we see in how God works in the small details of life? What does Os mean when he says there is often a trumpet call for each person's life?

What is one thing you will do because of what you learned in this chapter?

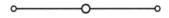

You will never know you are a giant killer until a giant attacks you. Life is about facing the giants in our lives. Change agents rarely grow up thinking they want to be change agents; rather, they are drafted into a conflict, then a calling and the larger story of their lives.

Identifying Your Six Stages
of the Joseph Calling

Now it's your turn. Perhaps you recognize in your own life the six stages God has brought you through in order to fulfill your Joseph calling. Or perhaps you are in the midst of one of the stages right now. Whatever the case, it is my desire that you would think about your life and the stages you see God has taken you through, or that he is presently taking you through. List them here. Describe the circumstances and what you have learned in each stage.

1. Recruitment: _____

_____

_____

_____

2. Character Development: _____

_____

_____

_____

3. Isolation: _____

_____

_____

_____

4. Betrayal: _____

_____

_____

_____

5. Problem Solving: _____

_____

_____

_____

6. Networks: _____

_____

_____

_____

If God is calling you into a Joseph calling, it will involve walking through these six steps to understand, navigate, and ultimately fulfill the call of God upon your life. Are you ready for your assignment?

About the Author

Os Hillman is president of Marketplace Leaders, an organization whose mission is to be a voice and agent to inspire, teach, and connect Christian believers to resources and relationships in order to manifest the life of Christ in their workplace call for cultural influence. Formally an advertising agency owner, Os is now an internationally recognized speaker on the subject of faith at work and a business owner. He is the author of eighteen books and a daily e-mail devotional called TGIF: Today God Is First, which has thousands of readers in over a hundred nations. He hosts a national radio show, Faith, Work, and Culture with Os Hillman, and has been featured on *CNBC*, *NBC*, the *LA Times*, and the *New York Times*.

Os is also founder and president of Aslan Group Publishing, which provides a leading online "faith-at-work" Christian bookstore called www.TGIFbookstore.com to serve the needs of Christians in their workplace and speaks to and trains leaders around the world. Os and his wife, Pamela, currently reside in north Atlanta. Os has a daughter and son-in-law that also live in the Atlanta area.

Please visit his websites to learn more:

www.MarketplaceLeaders.org

www.TodayGodIsFirst.com

www.MyChangeAgentNetwork.com

FOR MORE EQUIPPING

The Change Agent Network is an online equipping resource that features video teaching from Os Hillman, case studies, leader profiles, teleseminars and weekly teaching from Os Hillman. Receive a FREE membership at **MyChangeAgentNetwork.com**

OTHER BOOKS BY OS HILLMAN

Listening to the Father's Heart

TGIF: Today God Is First Devotional, Volume 1

TGIF: Today God Is First Devotional, Volume 2

Change Agent: How to Be the One Who Makes a Difference

*Experiencing the Father's Love: How to Live as Sons
and Daughters of Our Heavenly Father*

The 9 to 5 Window: How Faith Can Transform the Workplace

The Upside of Adversity: From the Pit to Greatness

Making Godly Decisions: How to Know and Do the Will of God

The Purposes of Money

Overcoming Hindrances to Fulfill Your Destiny

*The Faith@Work Movement:
What Every Pastor and Church Leader Should Know*

TGIF: Small Group Bible Study

Faith & Work: Do They Mix?

Proven Strategies for Business Success

So You Want to Write a Book

To learn more about these books, visit www.TGIFbookstore.com.

Made in the USA
Columbia, SC
18 September 2021